HIDEOUTS & TRAINING CAMPS

FIGHTING TERRORISM

David Baker

Rourke
Publishing LLC
Vero Beach, Florida 32964

www.rourkepublishing.com

PHOTO CREDITS: p. 24: Yasser Al-Zayyat/AFP/Getty Images; pp. 22, 23, 30 (SFC Thomas R), 39, 41: Department of Defense; p. 26: General Photographic Agency/Getty Images; p. 10: Getty Images; p. 5: Robert Harding World Imagery/Getty Images; p. 17: Chris Hondros/Getty Images; p. 8: Hulton Deutsch Collection/Corbis; p. 9: Keystone/Getty Images; p. 4: Ahmad Khateib/Getty Images; p. 20: Zubair Mir/AFP/Getty Images; p. 14 Georgi Nadezhdin/AFP/Getty Images; p. 18: Scott Peterson/Liaison/Getty Images; p. 28: Matthew Roberts/Getty Images; p. 6: Uriel Sinai/Getty Images; pp. 31 (Staff Sgt. Edward Holzapfel), 32 (Senior Airman Rebeca M. Luquin), 36 (b) (Staff Sgt. Jeremy T. Lock), 37 (Tech. Sgt. Efrain Gonzalez), 43 (Tech. Sgt. Brian Davidson): U.S. Air Force; pp. 38 (Staff Sgt. Bradley Rhen), 42 (Spc. Jerry T. Combes): U.S. Army; pp. 34 (Sgt. Andrew D. Pomykal), 36 (t) (Lance Cpl. Nathan E. Eason), 40 (Cpl. James L. Yarboro): U.S. Marine Corps; pp. 16, 33, 35 (Lieutenant Commander Christopher W. Chope): U.S. Navy; p. 13: Visual News/Getty Images; p. 25: Alex Wong/Getty Images

Title page picture shows a U.S. special agent checking an Afghan home for weapons.

Produced for Rourke Publishing by Discovery Books
Editor: Paul Humphrey
Designer: Ian Winton
Photo researcher: Rachel Tisdale

Library of Congress Cataloging-in-Publication Data

Baker, David, 1944-
    Hideouts and training camps / by David Baker.
        p. cm. -- (Fighting terrorism)
    Includes index.
    ISBN 1-59515-485-X
    1. Terrorists--Training of--Juvenile literature. 2.
Terrorism--Prevention--Juvenile literature. I. Title. II. Series.
    HV6431.B335 2006
    363.320973--dc22
                                    2005028007

Printed in the USA

TABLE OF CONTENTS

Chapter One

Secret Lives

A member of the Palestinian terrorist group Fatah in Gaza City, Gaza Strip. His mask helps conceal his identity.

Around the world free people in many places have come under attack from terrorists who believe they have a right to destroy the freedom of the individual. They believe, through religious or political **fanaticism**, that they have the right to change the way people choose to live their lives. They try to achieve this by terrorizing free people into submitting to their demands. They do this by attacks on civilian targets, by murder, and by taking hostages.

All this takes a lot of planning, organization, and control over the recruiting and training of those people expected to carry out such acts of violence and murder. They must hide, and they must have training camps for their recruits. They must lead very secret lives. Terror groups can form in countries anywhere. They must exist in secret because most countries reject terrorism. Some countries have vast areas of land where small groups are able to assemble without detection.

The rugged terrain of the Afghanistan-Pakistan border makes it an ideal place for terrorists to hide out.

The aftermath of a terrorist bomb attack in Beersheva, Israel, in August 2004. Many attacks of this sort are carried out by suicide bombers.

Terrorists planning attacks as individuals or groups do so at great risk to themselves. Very few countries support acts of violence and murder, especially when terrorist strikes are made against civilians and ordinary people going about their daily lives. Most countries work actively with international law enforcement officers and with various U.S. government agencies to detect and arrest terrorists or those planning attacks. Outlaws and terrorists alike know this and are aware that they can be hunted down at any time. If caught, these outlaws are brought to justice.

People who live outside the law need to hide their activities from law enforcement agencies. To avoid detection they have to cover their activities or hide their intentions by living apart from the rest of society. Most countries around the world work hard to root out terrorists, but the detection of terrorists and international lawbreakers can be difficult.

Chapter Two

Background to Terror

For many years law enforcement agents, police, and security staff have sought to combat terrorism. The fear that crime and terror could be exported to any country made it helpful to work collectively across state and national boundaries. Terrorists are not a new **phenomena**. They have been around for a very long time. Sometimes terrorists are called **freedom fighters** because they are trying to prevent the use of illegal force in their own countries.

There have been times since the end of World War II in 1945 that the United States and its allies have helped such groups fight oppression and torture in their own countries. In countries occupied by **Nazi** forces during World War II, the United States and its allies helped people liberate themselves from tyranny. In the decades following World War II, several countries in eastern Europe and Southeast Asia were controlled by **communists** taking their orders from the Soviet Union and China.

To combat the aggression and warlike intentions of international communism, the United States and its allies armed

Freedom fighter or terrorist? The U.S. supported French Resistance fighters like these against the occupying Nazi forces during World War II.

small countries so they could help themselves stave off these extreme pressures. As a result of this global threat from communism, the North Atlantic Treaty Organization (NATO) was formed in 1949. It was an alliance between the United States and a group of democratic countries in western Europe pledged to defend one another from any aggressive attack from a communist state, including the Soviet Union itself.

The pledge for countries to help themselves was declared in the name of a jet fighter aircraft bought by several NATO countries in the 1950s. Called "Freedom Fighter," it represented the spirited desire to rise against oppression. At one time the term "freedom fighter" applied to brave and bold efforts to fight

An early meeting of the North Atlantic Treaty Organization (NATO) in April 1950. The organization was set up to defend the post-war world against the threat of communism.

for freedom, liberty, and democracy. Over the last few years the phrase freedom fighter has been taken over by terrorists who attempt to claim a legitimate reason for their unlawful actions. This is why they are, for the most part, unable to find a natural home for their causes.

The attempts on their parts to disrupt normal life led by decent people in democratic states often results in terrorists having to flee the countries in which they were born.

All known terrorists to date have had problems with the countries of their birth. Terrorists do not always fight for their own countries but in other nations that they believe they can carry out a sufficient number of attacks. They do this to get publicity that can broadcast their grievances and get news reports talking about their cause. They also do it to attract other people who have similar views and who are looking for a group to join.

Terrorists can only work in groups if they are part of a coordinated band of like-minded people. It is for that reason that they seek places where they can hide, train, and plan specific attacks elsewhere around the world.

Terrorists can strike anywhere and then disappear. This train in Madrid, Spain, was blown up in March 2004.

Chapter Three

Training Camps for Terror

Places to set up camps and to train for attacks are not hard to find. There are many places around the world where small groups can hide undetected for long periods. In this way, leaders are created by their violent efforts and by publicity. Others are attracted by their vicious deeds and crimes.

Most terrorists are global migrants, people who move from country to country seeking hideaways as suitable locations. From remote regions they can gather people, materials, and resources to keep them alive and to provide time for the manufacture of bombs and **chemical agents** or to accumulate **biological toxins** for their attacks.

A typical example of a migrant terrorist is the infamous Osama bin Laden, the head of the Al Qaeda international terrorist network. The way he used several countries to achieve his terrorist aims and how he built camps and hideaways in several places is an excellent example of how a terrorist leader establishes a base and builds an organization.

Born to a rich Saudi Arabian family, bin Laden was opposed to the regime in his native country. He adopted an extreme form of

During this interview with a Pakistani journalist, Osama bin Laden (left) claimed he had nuclear and chemical weapons ready for use against U.S. targets.

his **Muslim** faith and used it to justify claims that non-Islamic foreigners were **infidels**—people without faith and therefore to be destroyed. This is not the teaching of **Islam** but it is adopted as a truth by extremists who seek to use religion for justifying terrorist acts. Bin Laden went to Afghanistan and fought against Russian troops after they invaded that country in 1979.

The Soviet Union had replaced the government of Afghanistan with one led by Najibullah, a man who was in

By 1989, Russian troops had been forced by Afghan fighters to withdraw from Afghanistan.

the pay of the communist Russians. Bin Laden fought against Najibullah. He did this because he believed that no Islamic country should have non-Islamic foreigners involved in their governing administrations. Afghanistan was a Muslim country and, apart from being guilty of an outright act of aggression, communist Soviet Russia was also a country that outlawed any form of religion. By fighting against the Russians, bin Laden believed he was doing the work of Allah, or God, in ridding the country of infidels.

For about 10 years bin Laden remained in Afghanistan, learning the tricks of staying alive in remote regions. From hidden locations he would join bands of armed freedom fighters intent on evicting the Soviets from the country. During the 1980s bin Laden scoured the mountains, rocky slopes, caves, and underground gullies that form so much of the countryside in Afghanistan. He lived off the land with other fighters and used weapons and explosives to attack Soviet troops.

When the Russians left and the communist regime of the Soviet Union began to collapse in 1990, bin Laden returned to his native Saudi Arabia. Within three years he had moved to Sudan, where he set up another base and wrote revolutionary letters and articles to magazines in the United States and Europe.

This bin Laden propaganda poster was found by U.S. troops in an Al Qaeda classroom in January 2004.

In 1996 bin Laden was forced to leave Sudan when he declared in an interview with a journalist that he had been living in that country for several years. Sudan could no longer deny his presence, and he fled back to Afghanistan. Knowledgeable of the country and its hidden areas where small groups could hide for very long periods without detection, bin Laden had the perfect place for building up a band of terrorists. Unseen and out of reach, he was given **asylum** by the Burhanuddin Rabbani government, then in power in the capital, Kabul.

His views were so explosive that bin Laden had not been allowed to remain in any other Muslim country. Neighboring Pakistan had only allowed him to cross its land if he went straight to Afghanistan and never came back. Finally in Afghanistan he began to construct a well-fortified camp at Tora Bora Agam, in what is known as the Nangarhar province. This area is between

Bin Laden and his terrorist fighters hid in underground caves like this one in the Tora Bora region of Afghanistan.

Taliban soldiers near Kabul, Afghanistan, in December 1999. The Taliban were ruthless rulers who deprived Afghanis of their civil rights and supported terrorist groups like Al Qaeda.

Kabul and Jalalabad, a region well known to bin Laden from his years spent fighting the Russians.

Once established at this first fortified camp, bin Laden used his considerable wealth to buy arms, weapons, and equipment necessary for a range of terrorist actions he planned to conduct against non-Islamic countries. From his hideout he drew in a large number of people volunteering to give their lives in the cause of extremism.

Communications equipment was laid, and international networks were set up to contact other groups with similar interests and to coordinate the supply of equipment. The Taliban, a group of religious fanatics, moved in to control Afghanistan, and bin Laden was given their protection.

When reports reached bin Laden through his extensive information sources that the Central Intelligence Agency (CIA) and the Federal Bureau of Investigation (FBI) were about to snatch him from his home in Jalalabad, he was quickly moved to Kandahar. This area, far to the southwest, became a second hideout, with armed guards provided by the Taliban. In addition, he had been allowed to keep 150 of his own Arab guards, and the new location became a fortress with access in and out through secret passages and tunnels.

Chapter Four

A Jihad against the United States and Israel

Bin Laden's continuous desire to publicize himself to the outside world was in contradiction of his need for a secret hideout. This was no obscure hole in the ground. He had all the resources that modern technology could provide, and he was eager to add new fortifications. Working with the Taliban, he built another ingeniously designed fortress in southern Khowst. This was closer to Kabul but now he had three locations in which to hide, none of which was easily accessible from the outside.

Because bin Laden had made substantial financial gifts to the Mujahideen groups, in their fight against the Russians, and to the Taliban, he was accepted and protected by them. His method of securing hideouts and making camps from them was to serve as a model for the Al Qaeda organization he would lead on terrorist activities around the world. Bin Laden's power base grew strong during 1998, and he openly publicized his encouragement for attacks on the United States and its allies around the world.

(Opposite) A fort in Khowst, eastern Afghanistan, where Osama bin Laden might have had his base.

In May 1998, from his fortified hideaway, bin Laden announced the formation of an "International Islamic Front For Jihad Against the United States and Israel." Four months later U.S. aircraft attacked the terrorist camps in Afghanistan, but much equipment and resources survived. Munitions and weapons were moved away through long interconnecting tunnels to storage dumps underground.

Communications equipment was taken to other places so that it would appear the arms had been smuggled elsewhere, diverting attention from their real location. Other camps had been set up to house the several hundred volunteers who went

In late 1998, U.S. forces began pounding suspected Al Qaeda hideouts in Afghanistan.

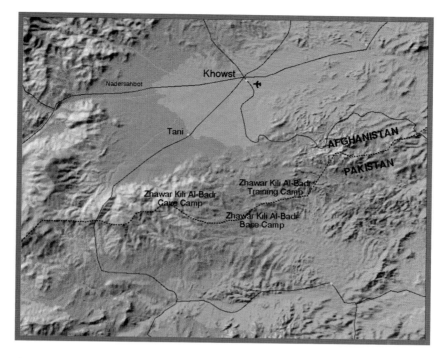

A U.S. Army map of the Khowst region of Afghanistan, showing the terrorist training camps, marked in red.

to Afghanistan as a result of bin Laden's frequent media appearances and use of televised recordings to broadcast his harmful message.

As groups began to merge with bin Laden, the numbers grew. Bin Laden's organization was known as the Harkat-ul-Jehad Al-Islami, and it was operating out of three camps in the Khowst region. Another camp, known as Salman Farsi, was situated at Jawah, less than 2 miles (3.2 km) from the border with Pakistan. Closest access was through the border post of Saidagi, and **infiltrators** would frequently hop across the border to get messages out of Afghanistan.

Bin Laden set up false trails to hide the true nature of these camps. Salman Farsi had been built in 1989 as a training facility

Members of Osama bin Laden's Al Qaeda terrorist group in training at the Al Farouq base in Afghanistan, June 2001.

for the Mujahideen and for Pakistani sympathizers jumping across the border. Two more camps were built for training suicide volunteers and for religious **indoctrination** on a daily basis. These were under the control of the Mujahideen, while the others were run exclusively by bin Laden and his fellow Arabs. The very essence of Al Qaeda—which means "The Base" —was that it should be a focus for a wide range of groups organized and managed by bin Laden. It was successful in that.

Al Qaeda trains its recruits to conceal themselves at several levels and to use hideouts, training camps, secret locations, and hidden arms dumps to operate in and out of countries without the knowledge of officials. Between 1998 and 2001, when the events of September 11 and the attacks on New York City and Washington, D.C. changed the world, bin Laden expanded the concept of operating bases from fortifications to urban hideaways.

In contrast with his mountain garrisons, bin Laden conceived the way in which members of his terrorist groups could hide for months, perhaps years, seeming to live and work as trusted colleagues right inside the countries targeted for attack. In a very real sense, these are as vital to his terrorist machine as the central mountain locations for organized group training.

Volunteers are important to the constant supply of new suicide bombers and terror killers. In some countries friends and family members are recruited. They are told they should commit

U.S. Attorney General John Ashcroft holds up a seized Al Qaeda training manual as he testifies at a Justice Department hearing on the war against terrorism, December 6, 2001.

their lives for their faith and that they have a duty to support other members of their family or group similarly involved.

Aware that terrorist volunteers were frequently committed religious fanatics with little or no knowledge of how to bomb, kill, or destroy buildings, Al Qaeda set up locations in Afghanistan to teach these people the basic operating methods involved. Volunteers would be recruited by word of mouth or by fanatical religious clerics in countries designated for attacks. They would make their own way to Afghanistan and, through a series of routes, enter the country through Pakistan or through the border with Russia.

Basic training in the methods used by Al Qaeda would be taught alongside lessons in the colonial powers that had controlled Arab and Islamic lands since the 19th century. Al Qaeda training manuals show the

Al Qaeda indoctrination includes teaching terrorists the history of western involvement in Muslim lands. This photo, from around 1922, shows British armored cars on patrol in the deserts of Iraq.

intense indoctrination in the history of conflict between Christians and Muslims that takes place at these camps.

The need to provide technical information is held back until a particular mission is planned and assigned to specific individuals. No one suicide volunteer knows anything other than what he or she is required to know to carry out the job. Al Qaeda works on the assumption that failed terrorists caught and interrogated will give away secrets vital to the organization, so they are told only as much as they need to know.

Training is adapted to changing patterns of activity. Some volunteers are told what is expected of them, and they are returned to their countries of origin where they can go immediately into preparations for an attack. Others are instructed to blend in with a new community in a different place than the one they lived in before training in Afghanistan.

Three levels of terrorist groups emerge from camps and recruiting places. One group is sent to recruit others and to arrange for willing sympathizers to contribute money for buying

FACT FILE ★

Many of the volunteers that came to join Al Qaeda were members of other terrorist groups with long histories of continuous attacks on U.S. and European interests in their own countries. Sometimes these volunteers were trained to infiltrate organizations to terrorize the general public. A terrorist attack can be a protest, but it is also used as a publicity notice to those who think these groups have been dismantled. Since Afghanistan, terrorist attacks have been made against targets in Spain, Britain, Indonesia, and other Southeast Asia countries.

Terrorists could be hiding anywhere. Here British police officers search a house in Leeds, in the north of England, following a terrorist attack in London on July 7, 2005.

weapons and arms. A second group is sent to link up with existing terrorist **cells** in specific countries. These cells are already assigned to a specific attack or to provide the resources for a series of attacks.

A third group is sent back to where it came from to remain silent and undetected for long periods of time waiting for a turn to be called upon. This group occupies what intelligence officials call "sleeper" cells, because people in this group appear to sleep until they are needed. These people can carry out normal work activities for an employer or, more likely, be kept by sympathizers to remain out of general contact from others in the local community.

Chapter Five

Attacks on the Hideaways

Since 9/11 Al Qaeda has had to regroup and restructure its activities. The events of that day brought a response the terrorists were unprepared for, as governments around the world supported a direct attack on camps in Afghanistan. While planning the greatest amount of damage they could achieve, interrogation of captured terrorists revealed that the organization did not expect to bring about the total collapse of the World Trade Center Twin Towers in New York City with the resulting loss of 3,000 lives. The sheer horror felt by decent people in many countries supported action the terrorists were not expecting.

For several months Al Qaeda adapted to the sustained pressure against them. Attacks against the terrorist groups were not only carried out by a combined military operation on places where their camps were located. Intelligence organizations in the United States and elsewhere also focused on rooting out sleeper cells and terrorists in their own communities. This has become an important part of stopping terrorist acts of violence. Hideaways and training camps are not only in central places that

At the Travis Air Base in California in October 2001, President George W. Bush stresses to the crowd that America "will not fail" in its war on terrorism.

can be identified and attacked, but they are also in towns and cities of the places targeted for attack.

Nevertheless, in response to 9/11 a major assault on the Taliban and Al Qaeda camps in Afghanistan was mounted by U.S. armed forces beginning in October 2001 with a series of bombing raids far greater in ferocity than anything previously launched against them. The mission was nicknamed "Operation

The attacks on the Twin Towers (opposite) and the Pentagon on September 11, 2001 brought Al Qaeda to the world's attention, and the world's response was swift.

A B-52H Stratofortress bomber taxis for takeoff on a strike mission against Al Qaeda training camps in Afghanistan, October 2001.

Enduring Freedom." The attacks came after the Taliban rejected demands from the U.S. government that Al Qaeda training camps and other hideouts and arms dumps in Afghanistan should be shut down and their occupants handed over. As the attacks intensified, the Taliban stiffened their resistance, and Al Qaeda leaders, together with bin Laden, took to tunnels and caves hidden from view to survive air raids and conserve their resources.

By December 2001 U.S. and **coalition** aircraft from several friendly countries including Great Britain began hammering at the main training complex at Tora Bora and around the Jalalabad and Kandahar regions. The training complex and its network of tunnels were bomb resistant due to the thick rock structure. Ground forces moved in on the structures half hidden from view in the sandy, dusty slopes of mountain passes and sunken ravines.

The tunnel complex was penetrated by armed fighters from dissident political factions in Afghanistan helped by U.S. advisers.

U.S and coalition forces invaded Afghanistan in October 2001. By January of the following year coalition forces had penetrated Al Qaeda munitions dumps, like this one in a cave in eastern Afghanistan.

Coalition forces in Afghanistan were aided by local anti-Taliban forces. Here Colonel Andrew P. Frick, of the 26th Marine Expeditionary, thanks Kandahar area Afghan commander Haji Gulali in January 2002.

U.S. and allied troops were there to provide support, bringing technical knowledge, equipment, and experience at fighting to a group struggling to save their own country from extremists. Combat air support was provided by the U.S. Navy, and F-18 Hornet and F-14 Tomcat strikes were made relentlessly against the terrorists.

The Tora Bora complex had been developed as a terrorist encampment after having been set up by the Mujahideen while they were fighting Soviet troops throughout the 1980s. Situated in a sunken valley, Tora Bora had numerous mountain passes and pathways where small groups of 10 to 15 men could literally walk out unseen.

A real problem for the allied forces was not knowing exactly where the underground tunnels, linking the interior of the camp to the outside, emerged. **Reconnaissance** pictures taken by overflying aircraft and by satellites in space helped pin down the

A U.S. Navy F/A-18 Hornet in the skies over Afghanistan, March 2002.

One of a series of tunnels found by the U.S. Marines in the Kandahar region of Afghanistan, January 2002.

locations of tunnels and caves but most remained hidden.

When they were found, some caves and tunnels showed details of impending attack from documents and maps that had been found in abandoned camps. Hurriedly departing in the face of sustained attacks, terrorists had left behind ample evidence of their murderous intent. Many future

When air raids on Afghan terrorist camps began in October 2001, the Department of Defense began dropping relief aid to refugees forced out of their homes by the Taliban. A message from President George Bush promised that while armed force would be used against the criminals, the "United States is a friend to the Afghan people." He went on to affirm that "The United States is an enemy of those who aid terrorists and of the barbaric criminals who profane a great religion by committing murder in its name."

attacks were aborted because the plans were discovered before they could be carried out.

Special equipment was needed to avoid booby traps and to carefully preserve evidence for trials that might take place if individuals were caught alive and brought to account for their crimes. Names, contacts, networks—gradually the picture began to build up from these finds scattered and hurriedly abandoned in these tunnels. Advanced and sophisticated means of

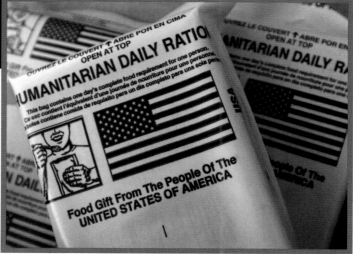

(Left) The inside of a C-17 Globemaster III loaded with humanitarian daily rations (right) to be dropped by the U.S. Air Force over Afghanistan.

detecting the presence of terrorists concealed in caves, tunnels or hideaways in the ground were employed.

Special "sniffing" devices were used to detect the presence of human beings down shafts in rock or in tunnels and caves. These devices can sense the odor given off by human breath or perspiration released as chemical particles into the surrounding atmosphere. They are so sophisticated that they can detect the presence of food eaten hours earlier by the odor on the breath of a human up to 250 feet (76 m) away. Some animals have this ability naturally. Dogs with a strong sense of smell are used by police and security personnel to detect illegal drugs.

Troops can find themselves in some pretty tight places when searching for weapons caches. Here, an infantry soldier is in operation in Wardak province in Afghanistan.

Chapter Six

High-tech Response

Cowering from their hunters, the men who would plan the deaths of thousands hid themselves and blended into the barren landscape but could not escape detection. Troops equipped with sniffer devices would carefully approach an area believed to shelter terrorists and obtain an "odor" map to identify pockets of human presence in the area. Even more advanced were sniffer devices carried by unmanned aerial vehicles (UAVs).

Looking like very large model airplanes, UAVs are operated remotely via a TV camera mounted in the nose by an operator who can be several miles away directing its flight from

Predator UAVs like this one have been used extensively in the skies over Afghanistan.

Marines on a mission to capture terrorists near Methar Lam, in Afghanistan, March 2005.

a TV screen. An example of this remotely controlled UAV is the Predator, which is equipped with sniffers, camera, sensors, or weapons. When they carry weapons to attack targets in dangerous areas, these flying machines are known as UCAVs—Unmanned Combat Air Vehicles.

At the time of the attacks on camps in Afghanistan at the end of 2001, the Defense Department had around 200 UAVs, building toward a current inventory of about 500. Threats to UAVs, and to their armed versions, would come from antiaircraft missiles, but it is to attack these threats to manned aircraft that they are used in areas where pilots' lives would be in great danger.

A more advanced UAV is the Global Hawk, larger than the Predator and able to fly to its own pre-designated target on instructions programmed into computers that hold it to a pre-determined track. Satellites and what the military call "space-based assets" are a great help in providing imaging for mapmakers to plot the flight path and signals for automated in-flight navigation.

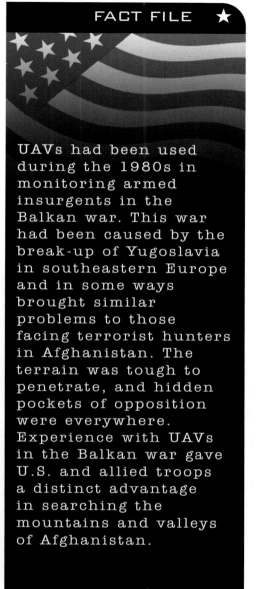

A surveillance satellite is launched into space from Cape Canaveral in Florida. Surveillance satellites have a critical role to play in finding terrorist training camps around the world.

Around the world, terrorists continue to hide from their pursuers. In the United States and Europe, every major capital city is a potential target for terror. Sleeper cells are known to exist in Britain, Germany, France, and Italy. This is why special units have been set up to hunt them down. Some countries employ special border police to keep out terrorists, some of whom claim to be seeking political asylum.

Throughout 2002 and into 2003 the business of searching caves and tunnels continued in parallel with the reconstruction of Afghanistan. U.S. and allied troops set to work building a new highway, giving aid to the hungry left aside by the Taliban, and flying in medical aid. Carried to the country by the threat from camps, training compounds, and tunnel complexes hiding large

Critical to the success of Operation Enduring Freedom has been the aid given to the local people. Here a U.S. Army doctor provides medical aid to a child in Kandahar province in Afghanistan.

The search for terrorist weapons goes on in Afghanistan. Here a U.S. special agent checks homes for suspected weapons caches.

stocks of weapons and munitions, U.S. forces were waging a secondary war. This war was for the hearts and minds of the confused and frightened innocent people of Afghanistan, themselves victims of the Taliban and extreme religious fanatics.

The war against terrorism is as much about encouraging democratic government by self-determination as it is by military force. By destroying Al Qaeda training camps, an important part of the terrorist campaign has been eliminated, but training goes on in different places. It exists in cities and in towns around the world, and it will probably never be completely eliminated. There will always be men and women waiting to kill and maim the innocent. The search for terrorists in camps and hideouts will continue in all those places and more.

Glossary

assassinate: to murder a very important person such as a president

asylum: when someone is given protection by a country other than his or her own

biological toxins: poisons that affect biological systems

cells: small groups of people

chemical agent: a substance that causes a chemical reaction

coalition: an alliance, often temporary, between people or nations

communist: a member of the communist party; someone who believes that the state should control the economy and government of a country

fanaticism: filled with great enthusiasm for a subject, e.g., a religion or belief

freedom fighter: a person who takes part in violent action to overthrow an oppressive government

indoctrination: attempting to influence people's beliefs and opinions

infidel: a person with no religious belief

infiltrators: people who secretly move into another country to spy and gain information

Islam: the religious faith of Muslims, which has Allah as the only God and Muhammad as His prophet

Muslim: a follower of the Islamic religion

Nazi: a member of the National Socialist German Workers' Party, the fascist party that ruled Germany during the 1930s and World War II

phenomenon: something that is very unusual or remarkable

reconnaissance: the exploration of an area often to gain military information

Further Reading

Binns, Tristan. *The CIA (Government Agencies)*. Sagebrush, 2002

Binns, Tristan. *The FBI (Government Agencies)*. Sagebrush, 2002

Brennan, Kristine. *The Chernobyl Nuclear Disaster (Great Disasters)*. Chelsea House, 2002

Campbell, Geoffrey A. *A Vulnerable America (Lucent Library of Homeland Security)*. Lucent, 2003

Donovan, Sandra. *How Government Works: Protecting America*. Lerner Publishing Group, 2004

Gow, Mary. *Attack on America: The Day the Twin Towers Collapsed (American Disasters)*. Enslow Publishers, 2002

Hasan, Tahara. *Anthrax Attacks Around the World (Terrorist Attacks)*. Rosen Publishing Group, 2003

Katz, Samuel M. *Global Counterstrike: International Counterterrorism (Terrorist Dossiers)*. Lerner Publishing Group, 2004

Katz, Samuel M. *Targeting Terror: Counterterrorist Raids (Terrorist Dossiers)*. Lerner Publishing Group, 2004

Katz, Samuel M. *U.S. Counterstrike: American Counterterrorism (Terrorist Dossiers)*. Lerner Publishing Group, 2004

Margulies, Phillip. *Al-Qaeda: Osama Bin Laden's Army of Terrorists (Inside the World's Most Infamous Terrorist Organizations)*. Rosen Publishing Group, 2003

Marquette, Scott. *America Under Attack (America at War)*. Rourke Publishing LLC, 2003

Morris, Neil. *The Atlas of Islam*. Barron's, 2003

Owen, David. *Hidden Secrets: A Complete History of Espionage and the Technology Used to Support It.* Firefly Books Ltd, 2002

Ritchie, Jason. *Iraq and the Fall of Saddam Hussein.* Oliver Press, 2003

Websites to visit

The Central Intelligence Agency:
www.cia.gov

The Department of Defense:
www.defenselink.mil

The Department of Homeland Security:
www.dhs.gov

The Federal Bureau of Investigation:
www.fbi.gov

The U.S. Air Force:
www.af.mil

The U.S. Army
www.army.mil

The U.S. Coast Guard:
www.uscg.mil

The U.S. Government Official Website:
www.firstgov.gov

The U.S. Marine Corps:
www.usmc.mil

The U.S. Navy:
www.navy.mil

The U.S. Secret Service:
www.secretservice.gov

The White House:
www.whitehouse.gov

Index